Vocabulary chart

Title	Vocabulary	Sounds	Bookband Level
World Instruments	from, girl, has, her, his, live, made, make, man, people, these, very, with		6 orange
Shapes	as, be, but, do, has, have, how, many, not, some, these, too, and number words: four, one, three	'll' (all) 'tr' (triangle) 'squ' (square) 'ng' (oblong)	7 turquoise
Shells	has, help, live, them their, these, with	''ll' (shell) 'rd' (hard) 'sn' (snail) 'pr' (protect) 'cr' (crab) 'cl' (clam)	4 blue
Night Animals	be, called, do, help, night, out, some, their, them, what, when, with	'sl' (sleep) 'sp' (special) 'sm' (small, smell)	5 green
From Curry to Rice	be, but, called, do, first, has, have, help, made, many, or, that, very, what, with, and colour words: black, brown, green, purple, red, white, yellow	'sp'	6 orange
Grandad and Me	an, brother, four, good, here, his, house, made, school, very, were, when, with, and colour words: brown, green, orange, white	'gr' (grandad)	5 green

Teaching objectives

	Teacher's Notes			Guided Reading Cards
	Speaking and listening	Reading	Writing	Reading
World Instruments				
Scotland	Listening/Talking Level A	Level A	Level A	Level A
N. Ireland	Activities a, f Outcomes a, c, e	Activities a, b Outcomes b, e, i	Opportunities a Outcomes b, d	Activities a, b Outcomes b, e, i Writing Outcomes b
Wales	Oracy Range 1, 3 Skills 2, 5, 6	Range 1, 2, 3, 4 Skills 1, 2 Language Development 2	Range 1, 3, 4 Skills 6	Range 1, 2, 3, 4 Skills 1, 2 Language Development 2 Writing Skills 6
NC/NLS Y1T2	1c 2d 3d	T17 T18 S6 W4	T22	T17 T23 S6 W3
Shapes				
Scotland	Listening/Talking Level A	Level A	Level A	Level A
N. Ireland	Activities a, f Outcomes b, c, d, e	Activities a, b Outcomes e, f, i	Opportunities a Outcomes b, d	Activities a, b Outcomes e, f, i Writing Outcomes b
Wales	Oracy Range 1, 3 Skills 3, 4, 5	Range 1, 2, 3 Skills 1, 2 Language Development 2	Range 1, 3, 4 Skills 6	Range 1, 2, 3 Skills 1, 2 Writing Skills 6
NC/NLS Y1T2	1d 2d 3a 3e	T2 T18 S2 S3 W3 W7	T23	T18 T23 S3 W7
Shells				
Scotland	Listening/Talking Level A	Level A	Level A	Level A
N. Ireland	Activities a, f Outcomes b, c, e	Activities a, b Outcomes b, c, e, i	Opportunities a Outcomes b, c	Activities a, b Outcomes b, c, e, i Writing Outcomes b, c
Wales	Oracy Range 1, 3 Skills 3, 4, 5	Range 1, 2, 3 Skills 1, 2 Language Development 2	Range 3, 4 Skills 5, 6	Range 1, 2, 3 Skills 1, 2 Writing Skills 5, 6
NC/NLS Y1T2	1d 2d 3a	T2 T17 T19 S2 S3 W6 W7	T25	T17 T25 S2 S3 W7
Night Animals				
Scotland	Listening/Talking Level A	Level A	Level A	Level A
N. Ireland	Activities a, f Outcomes b, c, d, e	Activities a, b Outcomes b, c, e, f, i	Opportunities a Outcomes b, c	Activities a, b Outcomes b, c, e, f, i Writing Outcomes b, c
Wales	Oracy Range 1, 3, 5 Skills 2, 4, 5	Range 1, 2, 3 Skills 1, 2 Language Development 2	Range 3, 4 Skills 5, 6	Range 1, 2, 3 Skills 1, 2 Writing Skills 5, 6
NC/NLS Y1T2	1b 1d 2d 3a 4a	T2 T18 S1 S3 W1 W7	T25	T18 T25 S6 W1

Fireflies
Stage 4
Gillian Howell

Teaching Notes

Contents

Introduction

Fireflies is an exciting non-fiction series within *Oxford Reading Tree*. The books are specially designed to be used alongside the Stage 1 stories. They provide practice of reading skills in a non-fiction context whilst using the same simple, repetitive sentences as the *Oxford Reading Tree* stories. They also contain a selection of high frequency vocabulary. Each stage builds on the reading skills and vocabulary from previous stages, and helps children to read with growing confidence. As children read these books, they should be encouraged to read independently through: using their knowledge of letter sounds; learning to recognize high frequency words on sight; using the pictures and the sense of the story to work out new vocabulary.

To help children approach each new book in this stage with confidence, prepare the children for reading by talking about the book, asking questions and using these Teacher's Notes and the additional *Guided Reading Cards* and *Take-Home Cards*.

How to introduce the books

Before reading the book, always read the title and talk about the picture on the cover. Go through the book together, looking at the pictures and talking about them. If there are words that are new or unfamiliar, point them out and read them with the children.

This booklet provides suggestions for using the books with groups of children or individuals. You can use the ideas with shared, group or guided reading sessions, or with individual children. Suggestions are also provided for writing, speaking and listening and cross-curricular links. You can use these suggestions to follow on from your reading, or use at another time.

Guided Reading Cards are available for each book. These provide more detailed guidance for using the books for guided reading. *Take-Home Cards* are also available for each book. These provide prompts and suggestions for parents reading with their children. You can store the relevant card with each book in your "Take-Home" selection of titles.

From Curry to Rice				
Scotland	Listening/Talking Level A	Level A	Level A	Level A
N. Ireland	Activities a, f Outcomes b, c, d, e	Activities a, b Outcomes c, e, f, h	Opportunities a Outcomes b, c	Activities a, b Outcomes c, e, f, h Writing Outcomes b, c
Wales	Oracy Range 1, 3 Skills 3, 4, 5	Range 1, 2, 3 Skills 1, 2, 3	Range 3, 4 Skills 5, 6	Range 1, 2, 3 Skills 1, 2, 3 Writing Skills 5, 6
NC/NLS Y1T2	1d 1b 2d 3a	T20 T21 S1 W7	T25	T21 T25 S1 W3
Grandad and Me				
Scotland	Listening/Talking Level A	Level A	Level A	Level A
N. Ireland	Activities a, f Outcomes a, c, d, e	Activities a, b Outcomes c, e, i	Opportunities a Outcomes b, c	Activities a, b Outcomes c, e, i Writing Outcomes b, c
Wales	Oracy Range 1, 3 Skills 3, 4, 5	Range 1, 2, 3 Skills 1, 2	Range 3, 4 Skills 5, 6, 7	Range 1, 2, 3 Skills 1, 2 Writing Skills 5, 6, 7
NC/NLS Y1T2	1d 2d 3a 3e	T2 T18 S2 S7 W6 W10	T24	T2 T24 S6 W3

World Instruments

Reading the book with individuals or guided reading groups

NB for additional and more detailed guidance on guided reading see Stage 4 Guided Reading Cards (available separately, ISBN 0199197598). Take-Home Cards are also available, providing guidance for parents/carers (ISBN 019919758X).

Introducing the book

- Look at the front cover. Ask the children what type of book this is going to be. Encourage them to look for clues, e.g. non-fiction because a photo is used to illustrate it.
- Ask the children to find the title, and read it with them.
- Discuss any instruments the children already know and what their purpose is, e.g. to make sounds for music.
- Look through the book and identify the different instruments being described on each page. Encourage the children to find the object words on the page.

During reading

- Encourage the children to read the book. Praise the children who read the repeated phrases confidently.
- Prompt the children to use the picture clues and initial sound to work out the new and unfamiliar words.

Observing Check that the children:

- understand the difference between the terms "fiction" and "non-fiction" (T17)
- understand that readers do not need to go from start to finish, but can select according to what is needed (T18)
- notice where sentences begin and end (S6)
- are confident when reading the high-frequency words "make" and "from" (W4)

After reading

- Ask the children to:
  Find the page that tells you where a steel drum comes from.
  Find the page that shows which instrument comes from Australia.

Group and independent reading activities

Text level work

Objective   To use terms "fiction" and "non-fiction", noting some of their differing features (T17)

- Ask the children to work with a partner and choose a storybook they have read recently.
- Ask them to look at the covers of both books, and look through the pages. Tell them to discuss how the non-fiction book is different from the story.
- Ask some of the pairs to explain their findings to the class.

Sentence level work

Objective   To use the term "sentence" appropriately to identify sentences in text, i.e. those demarcated by capital letters and full stops (S6)

Prepare:
The sentences and phrases below, written on a board, a computer or on pieces of paper:
This is a bagpipe.
A panpipe comes from Peru.
Steel drum West Indies
Saxophone United States of America
This girl is playing the panpipes.
Didgeridoo Australia

- Explain to the children that some of these groups of words are sentences, and some are not.
- Ask the children to put them into two groups.
- Encourage the children to say why some of the word groupings are not sentences, i.e. there is no full stop. Give extra praise to children who say that the phrases do not have verbs.

Word level work

Objective   To discriminate, read and spell words with initial consonant clusters "bl", "dr" and "pl" (W3)

- Write "blow" and "this" on the board and ask the children to read the words. Discuss the "bl" sound at the beginning of the word and explain that the two letters are consonants with separate sounds, while "th" is blended to make one sound.
- Ask the children to look through the book and find any other words that begin with two consonants that have separate sounds. (blow, drum, playing)

- Ask them to add other words from their own experience with the same beginnings.

Speaking and listening activities for groups

Objectives 1c) organize what they say; 2d) listen to others' reactions; 3d) extend their ideas in the light of discussion

Prepare: a selection of different instruments for the children to examine

- Ask the children to look at the instruments without touching them. Discuss with the children what the instruments' names are. In pairs, ask the children to say how they think the instruments will make a noise, using the language of the book, e.g. "You ......a ......to make music."
- Allow the children to test their ideas.

Cross-curricular links
◀▶ **Music (QCA Unit 2)**
Sounds interesting – exploring sounds; investigate how different instruments make different sounds
Geography (National Curriculum 3a)
Use the photographs and maps to find the places in an atlas or on a globe. Use evidence from the illustrations to speculate on what these places are like.
PSHE (Guidelines 4c)
Identify and respect the similarities and differences between people

Writing

Objective To write labels for drawings and diagrams (T22)

You will need:
a selection of instruments as a stimulus

- Encourage the children to experiment with the instruments to find out how they make sounds.
- Ask them to choose two instruments that are different, to draw the instruments and write a label on the drawing to say what they are.
- Ask them to write a sentence to say how they make music.

Shapes

Reading the book with individuals or guided reading groups

NB for additional and more detailed guidance on guided reading see Stage 4 Guided Reading Cards (available separately, ISBN 0199197598). Take-Home Cards are also available, providing guidance for parents/carers (ISBN 019919758X).

Introducing the book

- Look at the front cover. Ask the children what type of book this is going to be. Encourage them to look for clues on the front cover and by reading the back cover blurb together.
- Read the title together. Ask the children to say the names of shapes that they know.
- Look through the book with the children and read the headings together.

During reading

- Encourage the children to read the book. Praise the children who read the number words with fluency and confidence.
- Help children, who struggle with difficult words, to work them out by using the initial sounds and picture cues.
- Occasionally ask children to explain the information in their own words to ensure they understand the text.

Observing Check that the children:

- use a variety of approaches in working out new words (T2)
- predict words that make sense in the sentence (S2)
- are able to blend the phoneme "th" at the beginning of words, i.e. three, this, and at the end of words, i.e. length (W3)

After reading

Ask the children:
Can you find the pages that tell us about a triangle?
Can you find the pages that tell us about a cube?

Group and independent reading activities

Text level work

Objective To read non-fiction books and understand the reader doesn't need to go from start to finish (T18)

You will need:
a selection of shapes for the children to handle

- Ask the children to choose two or three shapes, and see if they can find information about them in the book.
- Ask them to draw the shapes, and write down what they found out from the text using complete sentences.

Sentence level work

Objective To predict words from preceding words in the sentences (S3)

Prepare: the sentences below, written on a board, a computer or on pieces of paper with missing words "have", "has", "are" and "is" written separately:

The opposite sides of a rectangle _____ the same length.
Some flat shapes _____ three sides.
This shape _____ three sides.
This cube _____ square faces.
It _____ a triangle.
The faces of this cuboid _____ rectangles.

- Ask the children to read the sentences and work out which word should go in the gap to make the sentences correct.
- Encourage them to use the book, if necessary. Encourage early finishers to find the sentence in the book. Praise the children who re-read the sentence to check if it makes sense.

Word level work

Objective To recognize the critical features of words, e.g. common spelling patterns (W7)

You will need: the word "shape" written on the board

- Cover the "e" and ask the children to read the word.
- Discuss how the "e" alters the sound of the vowel.
- Ask the children to look through the book and find other examples of words with long vowel sounds ending in "e".
- Ask them to add other similar words from their own experience to the list.

Speaking and listening activities for groups

Objectives 1d) focus on the main point; 2d) listen to others' reactions; 3a) take turns in speaking; 3e) give reasons for opinions

- With the children in a circle, ask them each to name something they see on their way to school, and to say what shape it is.
- Ask them to describe the shapes using the language of the book, e.g. the paving stone has four corners.

Cross-curricular links
◀▶ **Numeracy**
Framework Unit 5–6 Shape and space; Reasoning about shapes; Unit 10–11 Handling data
ICT (QCA 1D)
Labelling and classifying

Writing

Objective To produce extended captions (T23)

- Ask the children to look at the shapes they see around them in the classroom.
- Ask the children to describe one of the shapes, and to say how many sides/corners/faces it has.
- Ask them to choose three shapes, and to draw a picture of them, and write a sentence describing each one.

Shells

Reading the book with individuals or guided reading groups

NB for additional and more detailed guidance on guided reading see Stage 4 Guided Reading Cards (available separately, ISBN 0199197598). Take-Home Cards are also available, providing guidance for parents/carers (ISBN 019919758X).

Introducing the book

- Look at the front cover. Ask the children what type of book this is going to be, and to give a reason for their opinion, e.g. the cover has a photo to illustrate it.
- Ask the children to find and read the title.
- Ask them to look at the back cover, and read the blurb with them.
- Look through the book and ask the children to read the words in bold print.

During reading

- Encourage the children to read the book. Praise the children when they leave a gap and read on to predict new words.
- Prompt the children to use the picture clues and initial sound to work out the new and unfamiliar words.
- Ask the children, "Where is the snail?" etc. to help them read sentences with the words "inside" and "outside" fluently.

Observing Check that the children:

- use a range of strategies to help them work out words (T2)
- understand if their predictions about the content of the book were correct (T19)
- leave a gap and read on to help them predict words that fit in a sentence (S2)
- read the high frequency words on sight (W6)

After reading

- Read page 16 together and point to the word "clam". Ask the children to quickly skim through the book and find the pages that tell you about clams. Ask them to say how they found the pages, i.e. did they look for the word or the photograph?

Group and independent reading activities

Text level work

Objective To use the terms "fiction" and "non-fiction", noting some of their differing features (T17)

- Write two book titles on the board, "The Story of Simon the Snail" and "All about Snails".
- Ask the children:
  What do you think would be different about these two books?
- Encourage them to talk about the features of non-fiction texts, e.g. photographs, factual information.
- Ask the children to write a sentence to say what tells them that "Shells" is non-fiction.

Sentence level work

Objective To predict words from preceding words in sentences and investigate the sorts of words that fit, suggesting appropriate alternatives, i.e. that make sense (S3)

Prepare: the sentences below written on a board, a computer or on pieces of paper with the choice of words written separately alongside them:
A snail is inside _____ shell. this/those
It _____ a shell. has/have
The shell _____ with the turtle. moves/move

- Ask the children to read the sentences and work out which of the last words on each line should go in to make the sentences correct.
- Encourage early finishers to find the sentence in the book. Praise the children who re-read the sentence to check if it makes sense.

Word level work

Objective To recognize the critical features of words, e.g. words within words (W7)

- Write the word "inside" on the board. Ask the children to read the word, and break it into two syllables. Ask them to tell you what two small words make the longer compound word.
- Tell the children to look through the book and collect other examples of compound words. (sometimes, outside, cannot, without)
- Ask them to add other words to their list from their own experience, or by using a word bank or dictionary.

Speaking and listening activities for groups

Objectives 1d) focus on the main point; 2d) listen to others' reactions; 3a) take turns in speaking

You will need:
a selection of illustrated books about wildlife

- Ask the children to explain the purpose of the shells in the book "Shells".
- Ask them to suggest other animals that have hard "outsides" that help protect them.
- Ask them in pairs to look at the books about animals and collect a list of animals with protective bodies.
- Ask each pair to describe one of their findings for the rest of the class.

Cross-curricular links
◀▶ **ICT (QCA 1D)**
Labelling and classifying – use personal descriptions to describe objects

Writing

Objective To assemble information from own experience, to use simple sentences to describe, based on examples from reading, to write simple non-chronological reports (T25)

You will need:
a selection of illustrated books about animals

- Ask the children to select animals that have protective bodies, to be included in a book about how animals protect themselves.
- Draw up a list of the children's suggestions.
- Ask the children to suggest a sentence they could use to describe the animal.
- Scribe some of the children's suggestions, and together decide which one works best.
- Ask them each to choose one animal, to draw it and write a sentence to describe it.
- Collect the children's writing to put together for a class book.

Night Animals

Reading the book with individuals or guided reading groups

NB for additional and more detailed guidance on guided reading see Stage 4 Guided Reading Cards (available separately, ISBN 0199197598). Take-Home Cards are also available, providing guidance for parents/carers (ISBN 019919758X).

Introducing the book

- Look at the front cover and read the title with the children. Ask them what type of book they think this going to be. Together, read the back cover.
- Discuss with the children what sorts of animals are awake at night.
- Look through the book and identify some of the animals therein. Encourage the children to find the names on the page.

During reading

- Encourage the children to read the book. Praise the children who read the repeated word "nocturnal" with increasing confidence.
- Prompt the children to use the picture clues and initial sound to work out new and unfamiliar words.

Observing Check that the children:

- use more than one strategy to work out new words (T2)
- re-read sentences to check for sense (S1)
- can discriminate between the initial sounds of "night" and "light" (W1)

After reading

- Ask the children:
  What are animals called that wake up at night?
  Can you think of any other animals that are nocturnal?

Group and independent reading activities

Text level work

Objective To read non-fiction books and understand that the reader doesn't need to go from start to finish but selects according to what is needed (T18)

- Encourage the children to flick through the book to show you facts that they found interesting or new to them.
- Ask the children:
  Can you show me the page that tells us how bats find their food?
  What sort of things do mink eat?

Sentence level work

Objective To predict words from preceding words in sentences and investigate the sorts of words that "fit", suggesting appropriate alternatives, i.e. that make sense (S3)

Prepare:
The sentences below written on a board, a computer or on pieces of paper with a gap for the missing word:
Some animals wake _____ when it is dark at night.
Hedgehogs _____ for insects and worms to eat.
Some bats _____ nocturnal animals.
Kiwis smell out _____ food with their long beaks.

- Ask the children to read the sentences and think of a word to fit the gap.
- Tell them to read their sentences to a partner, to find the sentences in the book and compare their choice of word with the text and each other.

Word level work

Objective To recognize the critical features of words, e.g. common spelling patterns (W7)

- Look at the title of the book with the children and focus on the spelling of "Night".
- Ask the children to suggest other words with the same ending.
- Ask the children to look through the text and collect any other words with the same spelling pattern.
- Ask them to add words from their own experience to their list, and to look for others in a dictionary or word bank.

Speaking and listening activities for groups

Objectives 1b) choose words with precision; 1d) focus on the main point; 2d) listen to others' reactions; 3a) take turns in speaking; 4a) use language and actions to explore and convey situations

- Ask the children to work with a partner. Tell them to choose an animal from the book, to read the information about it, and work out how to mime what it does.
- Ask them to choose some words to say about the animal, e.g. Who am I? I eat insects and worms.
- Ask the children to perform their mimes for the rest of the class, and the other children guess the animal's name.

Cross-curricular links
◀▶ **IT (QCA 1D)**
Labelling and classifying – use personal descriptions to describe objects. Group animals according to different criteria, i.e. daytime/night-time animals
Science (QCA 1D)
Light and dark – explore the senses night animals use to find food

Writing

Objective To assemble information from own experience, e.g. daytime animals; to use simple sentences to describe, based on examples from reading (T25)

- Read pages 6 to 15 with the children, and discuss how one page tells you when the animal is awake, and the facing page tells you a fact about its food.
- Ask the children to think of some animals that are awake in the daytime, and draw up a list.
- Using one of their suggestions, write two sentences for the children to use as a model, based on the text.
- Ask them to choose an animal, draw it, and write two sentences about it using the model.
- Collect the pages to make a book on "Daytime Animals".

From Curry to Rice

Reading the book with individuals or guided reading groups

NB for additional and more detailed guidance on guided reading see Stage 4 Guided Reading Cards (available separately, ISBN 0199197598). Take-Home Cards are also available, providing guidance for parents/carers (ISBN 019919758X).

Introducing the book

- Look at the front cover. Ask the children what type of book they think this is going to be. Read the title together, and the back cover blurb.
- Ask the children to suggest food that might be in the book.
- Ask them to look at the index on page 16 to see if their suggestions are included.

During reading

- Ask the children to read the contents page, and encourage them to read the book. Praise the children who break longer words into syllables to work them out.
- Prompt the children to use the picture clues and initial sound to work out the new and unfamiliar words.

Observing Check that the children:

- understand the alphabetical organization of dictionaries and encyclopedias (T20)
- predict words they are unsure about by trying words that fit and re-reading for sense (S3)
- recognize the smaller words within compound words (W7)

After reading

- Ask the children:
  Can you tell me a way to find the page about ice cream?
  Can you quickly find rice in the book?

Group and independent reading activities

Text level work

Objective To understand the purpose of contents pages and indexes and to begin to locate information by page numbers and words by initial letter (T21)

You will need: word cards of the foods detailed in *From Curry to Rice*

● Ask the children to work with a partner.
● Tell the children to take turns to pick a word card, then ask their partner to find out one fact about the food on the card.

Sentence level work

To expect reading to make sense, and check if it does not (S1)

Prepare:
the sentences below written on a board, a computer or on pieces of paper with missing words written separately:

_____ can be round with a hole in the middle.
_____ are smooth purple vegetables.
_____ can be purple or green.
_____ has a sweet taste.
_____ are big yellow and red fruits.
_____ can be white, black or brown.
Doughnuts, Eggplants, Grapes, Ice-cream, Mangos, Rice

● Ask the children to read the sentences and work out which word should go at the beginning of each sentence to make sense.
● Encourage them to use the book, if necessary. Guide early finishers to find the sentence in the book. Praise the children who re-read the sentence to check if it makes sense.

Word level work

Objective To recognize the critical features of words, e.g. words within words (W7)

● Write "grown" on the board. Demonstrate for the children how to find other words within this word, i.e. grow, row, own.
● Write "vegetable" on the board. Ask the children to find three new words in this word, i.e. get, table, able.
● Ask the children to read the text and collect other examples of words within words.
● Choose some children to read the words they found to the rest of the class.

Speaking and listening activities for groups

Objectives 1d) focus on the main point; 1b) choose words with precision; 2d) listen to others' reactions; 3a) take turns in speaking

- With the children in a circle, ask the children to add other foods to the alphabet starting with A. When no more foods can be thought of, move to the next letter.
- The children could play the game cumulatively, e.g. I went to the market and I bought, apples, artichokes, asparagus, bananas, beans, butter etc.

Cross-curricular links
◀▶ ICT (QCA 1D)
Labelling and classifying – use personal descriptions to describe objects, sorting into sub-sets

Writing

Objective To assemble information from own experience, e.g. food, to use simple sentences to describe, based on examples from reading (T25)

- Together draw up a list of other foods beginning with each letter of the alphabet.
- Ask the children to write the name of the food, and one fact about it, and to draw a picture of it.
- Collect the children's work and arrange it in alphabetical order to make a class Food encyclopedia.

Grandad and Me

Reading the book with individuals or guided reading groups

NB for additional and more detailed guidance on guided reading see Stage 4 Guided Reading Cards (available separately, ISBN 0199197598). Take-Home Cards are also available, providing guidance for parents/carers (ISBN 019919758X).

Introducing the book

● Look at the front cover. Ask the children what type of book this is going to be.
● Ask the children to read the title. Are there any words they can recognize in the title? ("me" or "and") Read the back cover blurb with the children. Discuss the idea that the book is not about them but it is about the child who is talking about "me".
● Look through the book and identify the comparisons that are being made. Encourage the children to find these words on the page, e.g. school, house.

During reading

● Encourage the children to read the book. Praise the children who read the repeated words and phrases fluently.
● Prompt the children to use the picture clues and initial sound to work out the new and unfamiliar words.

Observing   Check that the children:

■ use a range of strategies to work out new words (T2)
■ expect the sentences to make sense and re-read them if they do not (S2)
■ read the familiar high frequency words with confidence (W6)

After reading

● Ask the children:
What things are the same for Grandad and the child in the book?
What things are different?

Group and independent reading activities

Text level work

Objective   To read non-fiction books and understand that the reader doesn't need to go from start to finish, but selects according to what is needed (T18)

You will need:
the following word cards as a stimulus:
school, house, ice cream, toy, cricket, car

- Ask the children to work with a partner, and pick a word card at random. The children swap their word cards and flick through the book to find the information about the topic and read it to their partner.

Sentence level work

Objective   To use capital letters for the personal pronoun "I", for names and for the start of a sentence (S7)

- Discuss the information about the child in the book with the children.
- Ask them to choose three of the topics from the book, e.g. homes, toys, cars, and to write a sentence about themselves for each topic.
- Remind the children to use capital letters and full stops.

Word level work

Objective   New words from reading and shared experiences and to make collections of personal interest or significant words and words linked to particular topics (W10)

You will need:
the following word cards:
photo, wafer, cone, cricket, sailing boat, computer game

- Ask the children to match the words with the correct page where they find the information in the book.
- Encourage the children to use the initial (and final) phoneme to work out the new words. Praise the children who remembered the words featured in the book and read them confidently.

Speaking and listening activities for groups

Objectives 1d) focus on the main point; 2d) listen to others' reactions; 3a) take turns in speaking; 3e) give reasons for opinions

You will need:
pictures or photos of children from different eras in the past and from the present

- Allow the children time to look at the pictures themselves. Encourage them to look closely at the clothes, and the backgrounds.
- Ask the children to describe the appearances of some of the children.
- Ask them to say what they like or dislike about the different clothing.
- Ask them which type of clothing they would like to wear and why.

Cross-curricular links
◀▶ **History (QCA 1)**
How are our toys different from those in the past? – identify old and new objects; handle and talk about their own toys and toys in the past; identify some differences between old toys and new toys
History (QCA 2)
What were homes like in the past? – collect pictures of old and new homes and compare
ICT (QCA 1D)
Labelling and classifying – use personal descriptions to describe objects

Writing

Objective To write simple questions (T24)

- Ask the children some questions about the Grandad in the book, e.g. "What toy does Grandad like?"
- Discuss what sort of words to use to begin questions and write them on the board.
- Ask the children to write four questions each and swap them with a partner.
- Tell the children to read their partner's questions and to answer them orally.

Links to other Oxford Reading Tree titles

Fireflies Stage 4	Oxford Reading Tree stories with similar subjects/themes
World Instruments	The Headache, The Band, The Carnival, The Play, The Dragon Dance, The Wedding
Shapes	The Big Box, The Balloon, The Flying Elephant,
Shells	Creepy-crawly! What is it?, Lucky the Goat, Pip and the Little Monkey, Jo and the Mouse, A Cat in the Tree, Book Week, Roy and the Budgie, Pip at the Zoo, The Little Dragon, Monkey Tricks, The Lost Puppy
Night Animals	Creepy-Crawly! What is it?, Lucky the Goat, Pip and the Little Monkey, Jo and the Mouse, A Cat in the Tree, Book Week, Roy and the Budgie, Pip at the Zoo, The Little Dragon, Monkey Tricks, The Lost Puppy
From Curry to Rice	Strawberry Jam, The Barbecue, Jan and the Chocolate, Lucky the Goat, The Toy's Party, The Wedding, Roy at the Fun Park, Midge and the Eggs,
Grandad and Me	Roy at the Fun Park, Village in the Snow, Gran, Castle Adventure, A Monster Mistake, The Great Race

OXFORD
UNIVERSITY PRESS

Great Clarendon Street, Oxford OX2 6DP

Oxford University Press is a department of the University of Oxford. It furthers the University's objective of excellence in research, scholarship, and education by publishing worldwide in

Oxford New York

Auckland Bangkok Buenos Aires Cape Town Chennai Dar es Salaam Delhi Hong Kong Istanbul Karachi Kolkata Kuala Lumpur Madrid Melbourne Mexico City Mumbai Nairobi São Paulo Shanghai Taipei Tokyo Toronto

Oxford is a registered trade mark of Oxford University Press in the UK and in certain other countries

© Oxford University Press 2003

The moral rights of the author have been asserted

Database right Oxford University Press (maker)

First published 2003

British Library Cataloguing in Publication Data

Data available

Teacher's Notes: ISBN 0 19 919757 1

10 9 8 7 6 5 4 3 2 1

Page make-up by IFA Design Ltd, Plymouth, Devon

Printed in China through Colorcraft Ltd., Hong Kong